ROYAL ACADEMY ILLUSTRATED 2002

'The most beautiful thing we can experience is the mysterious'
Albert Einstein

ROYAL ACADEMY ILLUSTRATED 2002

A selection from the
234th Summer Exhibition

Edited by Alison Wilding RA

Royal
Academy
of Arts

SPONSORED BY

ATKEARNEY
an EDS company

Acknowledgements

The task of the 'chief curator' of the Summer Exhibition is a considerable one which is only made possible by the support of a large team.

I firstly would like to thank the President and my fellow Council members for their advice and contribution to this year's exhibition. Among the Academy's staff I would like to thank the Membership and Summer Exhibition Department for all their help and support. The Art Handlers and their team need a special mention, as do the Press, Marketing and Publications departments for their essential contribution to the exhibition.

I would particularly like to thank Gary Hume RA for his invited room, and Edith Devaney, who has been instrumental in every aspect of the exhibition. *Bryan Kneale RA*

Contents

Sponsor's Preface

The symbiotic relationship between the arts and business is instantly recognisable in the world around us – from Warhol's depiction of Campbell's Soup cans to product placement in films. A.T. Kearney's continued sponsorship of the Summer Exhibition is an example of this tradition which includes some of the great works and great artists of our time.

Our involvement in the world's largest open contemporary art exhibition is a great source of pride, not just for A.T. Kearney, but also for our clients and partners across the globe who view this as a tangible example of our commitment to the arts.

It also goes some way to underline the other arts programmes A.T. Kearney is involved in, including our own initiative, 'Portraits of Business', whereby each year we commission four Royal Academicians to paint their impressions of four of our leading multi-national clients, thus inspiring greater dialogue between arts and business. Every year, these works are hung at the entrance to the Summer Exhibition.

Each new work by these artists is an example of how we all view things differently, influenced by our own personal experiences, backgrounds and system of beliefs. Similarly, in our work as management consultants, we find successful delivery of results depends on an understanding of the unique skills and individual cultures of our clients.

So, with this, the 234th Royal Academy Summer Exhibition, let me take this opportunity to express my hope that the hundred thousand people expected to walk the floors of this year's Exhibition take away just a small fraction of the enthusiasm that A.T. Kearney put into our sponsorship of it.

Carl Hanson
UK Managing Director

ATKEARNEY
an EDS company

Introduction

This year's Summer Exhibition sees a special and particular focus on sculpture. Determined by the date of his election (1970), Bryan Kneale is the most senior RA on Council, so he automatically became the chief curator of the show, known as the 'Senior Hanger'. As he says, 'we haven't had a Senior Hanger who was a sculptor in living memory, so it was a great opportunity to pull out all the stops for sculpture. The editor of the *Illustrated* this year is also a sculptor, Alison Wilding, and word has got around. We've just finished restoring the courtyard, so we'll have several major pieces of sculpture outside which will link up to the sculpture inside.

'The exhibition as a whole follows the novel and revolutionary ideas implemented by last year's Senior Hanger, Peter Blake. He separated Academicians from non-Academicians and chose a roomful of work by artists he invited to show. We've taken his formula and given it a good shake in the direction of sculpture. In painting, Academicians are separated from non-Academicians, but in sculpture they're mixed. We've got some very good pieces and there's a lot of variety in scale and idea.

'This year Norman Rosenthal, the Exhibitions Secretary, was invited to help with the hanging of Galleries I, II and III. He's also helped Gary Hume with his room of invited artists. Gary's a newly elected Academician and he's also the youngest. It seemed a good idea to give the room of invited artists to a new member who's got a new idea of the Academy. He's worked extremely hard. Of course we start work on the Summer Exhibition well before Christmas, visiting artists and informing art schools.

'The send-in this year? It's the usual extraordinary collection of work. Looking at thousands of paintings, drawings and pieces of sculpture can be traumatising. I haven't slept much since the process began: it's impossible to switch off all those images. It's totally different from the way you live normally as an artist where you're concentrating on your own work. You have to try to get under the skin of the artists you're looking at and imagine their works in the context of others. It's very different from hanging an exhibition of one or a limited number of artists you know well. You're dealing with a whole series of problems simultaneously. The RA's Victorian galleries, now perfectly restored, need to be thought about properly. Even when there's nothing in them, they have a personality. So we make adjustments to accommodate the work that comes in.

'It's a most enjoyable and very exciting business getting the show together because of the changes that happen as the pieces go up. It's extremely satisfying getting something in the right place. We could really do with more galleries for the Summer Exhibition – then we'd be able to include more and give more space to each exhibit. Perhaps we will when we finally get into the Museum of Mankind.'

Prof. Bryan Kneale RA
Horizon
Aluminium and copper
H 60 cm

Gallery I

This year Gallery I is hung solely with Academicians' abstract work. Usually the Honorary RAs are featured here, and the gallery is hung by the President. But this year, in a refreshing break with tradition, Galleries I, II and III have been allocated entirely to the Academicians, and the work has been hung by Maurice Cockrill in collaboration with Norman Rosenthal; the latter celebrating 25 years at the RA with his first ever involvement in the Summer Exhibition. Around the walls are works by six painters, beautifully hung. In the middle of the floor is the colourful mixed-media sculpture *And did those hills...* by Phillip King, which masterfully balances the geometrical figures of circle, square and triangle against the organic elements of pigment, slate pebbles, hay and feathers (detail opposite). As Alison Wilding remarks, 'This work draws the whole gallery together, and it's quite extraordinary how it pulls it off.' As Wilding says, the sculpture is completely at ease with the paintings around the walls, which represent in effect a tribute to British abstraction. Three powerful paintings by Sandra Blow, their surfaces animated not only by striking chords of colour but also with a collage of hessian, canvas and corrugated paper, set a pace which is maintained by a vibrant and predominantly pink triptych by Gillian Ayres and the two dramatic sentinel images by John Hoyland which flank the entrance to Gallery II.

Sandra Blow RA
Red Square
Mixed media
244 × 244 cm

Prof. Phillip King CBE, PRA
And did those hills...
Mixed media
H 120 cm

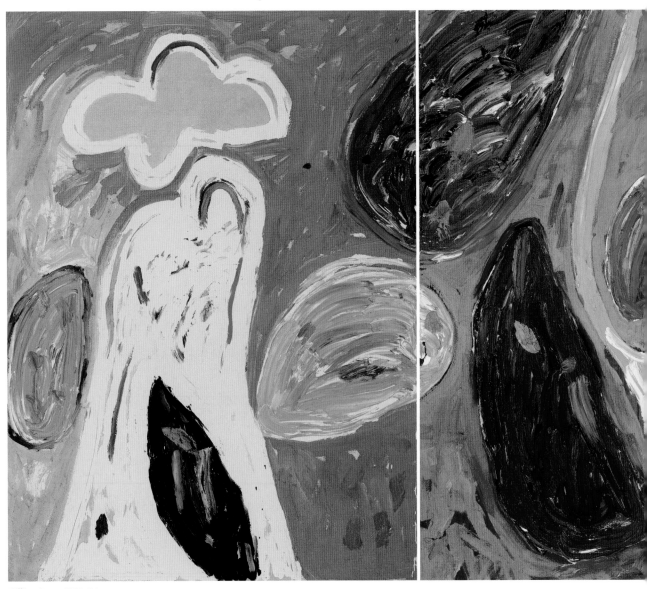

Gillian Ayres OBE, RA
Ankh 2000 (triptych)
Oil
152 × 548 cm

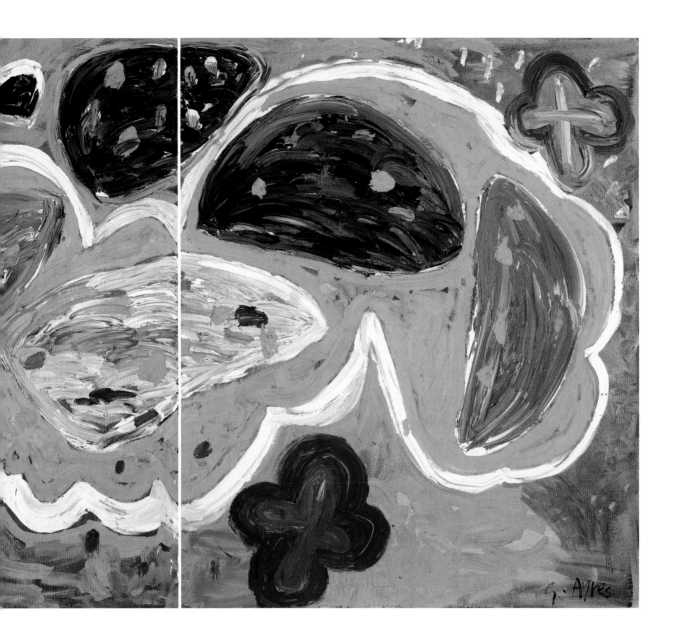

Prof. John Hoyland RA
Wanderer's Song 3.4.2002
Acrylic
254 × 233 cm

Albert Irvin RA
Schubert 2002
Acrylic
213 × 305 cm

Gallery II

The spare and elegant hang continues in Gallery II. 'It's quite sombre, this space,' comments Wilding. 'I particularly like the wall of Maurice Cockrill's and Kyffin Williams's paintings. They're such disparate artists yet their work really succeeds hanging together' (detail opposite). To the left, there's a memorial display of watercolours of Italy, Portugal and Majorca by Paul Hogarth, illustrious traveller and illustrator, who died last December. Next to them, and darkly glowing, are three small near-abstract Stations of the Cross by Norman Adams. By contrast the opposite wall is densely hung with small paintings by Bernard Dunstan, Diana Armfield, Leonard Rosoman and Patrick Procktor. Maurice Cockrill calls it 'a corner of intimacy. When you move in and see things from a different viewing distance, you see worlds in close focus, full of grace and gentleness.' Wilding praises the awkward yet vital quality of Procktor's drawing. Rosoman includes four acrylic studies of himself at work in Lambeth Palace Chapel. Four fragmented, poetic paintings by Sonia Lawson hang opposite a wall of greenhouse landscapes by Olwyn Bowey. 'There's an intimacy with nature here which is totally authentic and convincing,' comments Cockrill. The Lawsons look as if they are packed with references: one – *Verona II* – reminds Wilding of Rembrandt's *Polish Rider*.

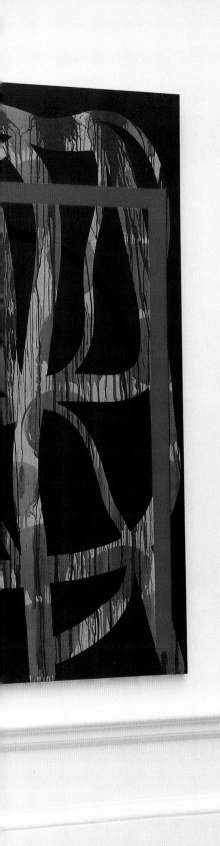

Diana Armfield RA
Later Summer Flowers
Oil
30 × 25 cm

Patrick Procktor RA
Wicker Chair
Oil and charcoal
66 × 44 cm

James Butler RA
Girl Dancing
Bronze
H 41 cm

Bernard Dunstan RA
Rehearsal II – The Harp
Oil
24 × 25 cm

Maurice Cockrill RA
Gold Fire Bridge
Acrylic and oil
150 × 180 cm

Sir Kyffin Williams OBE, RA
Evan Roberts
Oil
125 × 74 cm

Ken Howard RA
Dora, Venice Interior
Oil
122 × 102 cm

Olwyn Bowey RA
Old Oak Tree at West Dean
Gouache
78 × 98 cm

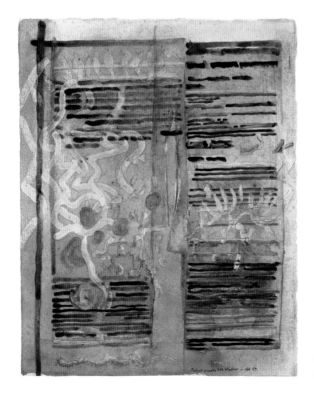

Prof. Norman Adams RA
The Fourth Station: Jesus and His Mother
Watercolour
44 × 34 cm

Leonard Rosoman OBE, RA
Self-portrait, Florence
Acrylic
17 × 28 cm

Paul Hogarth RA
Palazzo Sansedoni, Siena
Watercolour
50 × 40 cm

Large Weston Room

As so often in previous years, this gallery is dedicated to prints and works on paper by both Academicians and non-Members, worked in a wide variety of styles and techniques. For instance, compare the bold linocuts of Eileen Cooper with the more delicate surface of Stephen Chambers's etching of a fisherman. Mark Karasick makes a more enigmatic image with litho and encaustic. Barbara Rae contributes a large and vibrant silkscreen. There are two subtle hand-toned photographs by Jean Macalpine, while Tom Phillips has put through the computer four of the thousands of postcards he has collected, and made them into large silkscreen prints. Alison Wilding singles out the work of Ian McKeever for comment. He is represented by two etchings entitled *Between Space and Time Nos 8 and 9*. 'I'm drawn to that dark mass with its strange pink background, whether it's a void or a mass you don't really know. And the other one, with its idea of water. They're very *present* as objects.' On the adjacent wall are three Lambda prints on canvas by Julian Opie of fruit still-lifes. 'They're very blank but strong images,' comments Wilding. Nearby hang two Kitaj lithographic drawings. A pair of direct and textural Basil Beattie monoprints contrast with four small Craigie Aitchison screenprints with saturated colours and deckled edges. Wilding likes the exquisitely rendered, coloured-pencil dog portraits by Chrissy Wilson. 'Animals are very problematic, aren't they? At least these aren't sentimental.' Three Frank Auerbach etchings done with his typically taut and nervy line sound a different note. 'I like the relationship between that etched head and Bill Tucker's great sculptured head like a meteorite in Gallery IX,' says Wilding. A small black-and-white screenprint of fish on an oval platter by Patrick Caulfield makes a good contrast; 'incredibly elegant', comments Wilding.

STANLEY ROAD

The Roads Also by Wilfred Ow

The roads also have their wistful rest,
When the weathercocks perch still and roost,
And the town is a candle-lit room—
The streets also dream their dream.

The old houses muse of the old days
And their fond trees leaning on them doz
On their steps chatter and clatter stops,

Peter Blake.

109   PARIS
Tour Eiffel avec la Seine

Chrissy Wilson
Texas
Pencil
36 × 27 cm

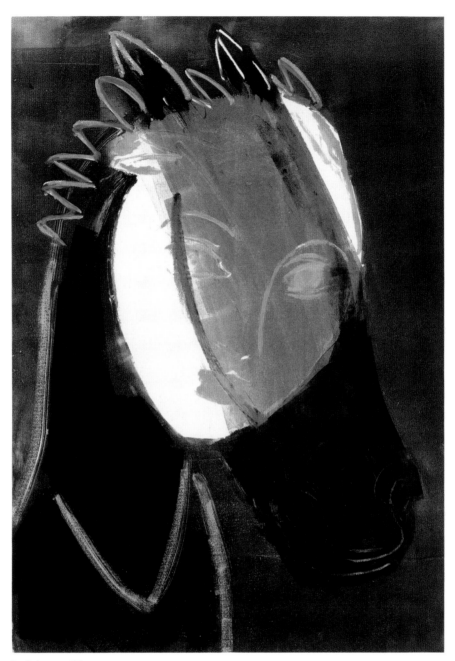

Sonia Lawson RA
Girl Dreams of Pony
Silkscreen
60 × 43 cm

Basil Beattie
That Irresistible Climb 7
Monoprint
40 × 50 cm

Basil Beattie
That Irresistible Climb 14
Monoprint
40 × 50 cm

Barbara Rae CBE, RA
Carrowtiege
Mixed media
96 × 107 cm

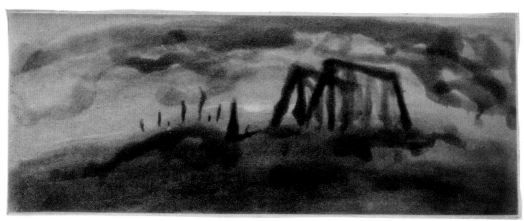

Nick Richards
The Bridge
Etching
10 × 24 cm

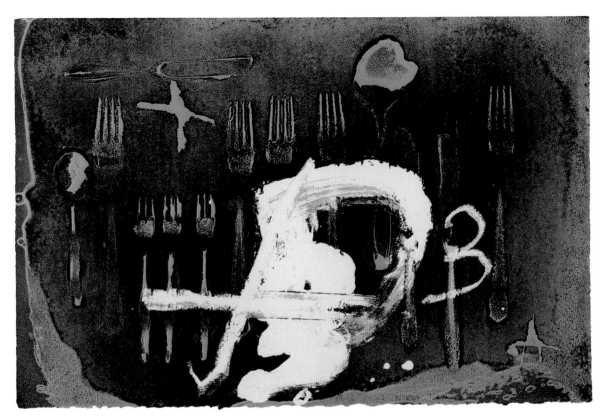

Antoni Tàpies
Coberts 3, 1993-4
Etching
33 × 50 cm

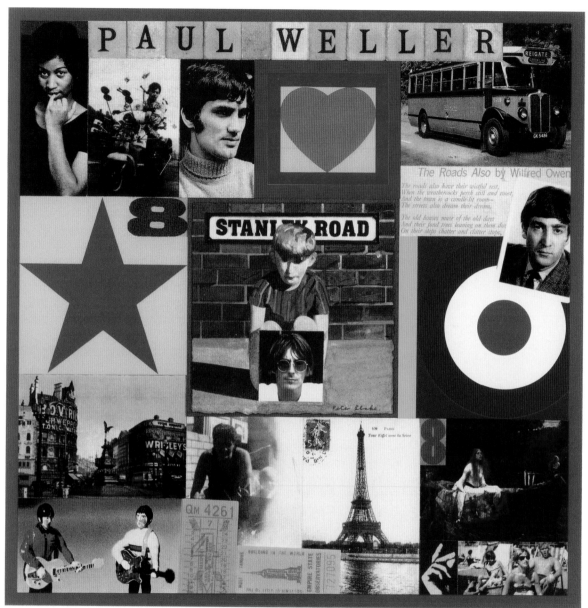

Peter Blake CBE, RA
Stanley Road
Silkscreen
47 × 47 cm

Julian Opie

Still-life with Bananas,
Aubergines and Green Beans
Lambda print
39 × 64 cm

Still-life with Green and
Red Apples
Lambda print
39 × 64 cm

Still-life with Orange,
Grapes and Red Apple
Lambda print
39 × 64 cm

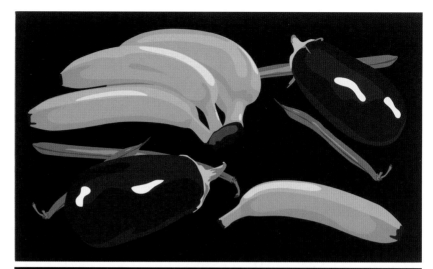

Patrick Caulfield RA
Brown Pot
Screenprint
74 × 52 cm

Prof. Paul Huxley RA
Jeu de Cartes
Silkscreen
36 × 36 cm

Quentin Blake
Drawing with Birds 3
Crayon
57 × 76 cm

Ralph Brown RA
Reclining Figure Europa
Charcoal
32 × 45 cm

Craigie Aitchison CBE, RA
Candy Dead
Screenprint
30 × 25 cm

Sir Terry Frost RA
Vertical Rhythms
Silkscreen
72 × 70 cm

Prof. Chris Orr RA
Green Rocks under St Petersburg
Silkscreen
69 × 102 cm

Ian McKeever
Between Space and Time No. 9
Etching
36 × 49 cm

Ian McKeever
Between Space and Time No. 8
Etching
37 × 50 cm

Tom Phillips RA
We Are the People No.12. The Bride.
Sheffield c. 1922
Epson and silkscreen
40 × 62 cm

Dr. Jennifer Dickson RA
Petal Screen, Milton Lodge
Giclée print
34 × 46 cm

Bill Jacklin RA
Westminster Dog Show I
Monoprint
12 × 14 cm

Victoria Crowe
*Drawn from Nature:
Young Jackdaw*
Print
16 × 21 cm

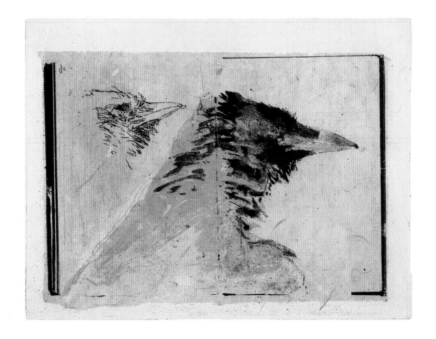

Peter Freeth RA
A Landscape with Figures
Aquatint
50 × 59 cm

Patrick Caulfield RA
Two Fish on a Plate
Lithograph
20 × 24 cm

David Hockney CH, RA
Dog Etching No. 14
Etching
21 × 27 cm

Frank Auerbach
Julia Asleep
Etching
20 × 25 cm

Cheryl Aaron
Studio Landscape
Print
9 × 12 cm

Gerard Hemsworth
Rabbit with Flowers
Print
60 × 59 cm

Small Weston Room

This year Allen Jones is the Summer Exhibition's featured artist, and as such is allotted this gallery for a solo show. A painter who also sculpts, deriving most of his sculptural ideas from his paintings, Jones has created a mixed-media installation of paintings, drawings, photographs and sculptures. Approaching the gallery you encounter a luminous red woman, internally lit, walking parallel to you. Another similar figure in orange walks away. A third sculpture is of a female figure in green containing a small refrigerator. These figures signal a return in Jones's work to the furniture sculptures he made in 1969–70, when he first tried to make a functional three-dimensional image that wasn't fine art sculpture. Essentially, two of the figures function as lights and the third as a drinks cabinet. Two large rectangular paintings nearby investigate a favourite Jones theme: the artist and muse. By juxtaposing the three-dimensional with the two-dimensional in this way, Jones illuminates the artifice of painting, while four small images trace the genesis of the sculptures back to a photograph he took in 1965 of a show-girl slot machine in Reno, Nevada.

Allen Jones RA
The Dance Academy
Oil
152 × 273 cm

Gallery III

In this gallery, Academicians' work has been mostly kept together and hung densely but 'harmoniously' (Rosenthal's word) in blocks around the walls. Usually the larger paintings are reserved for this room, but this year they are hung in Galleries I and II, and Gallery III has more small works. Wilding comments: 'It's very risky really, a brave way of getting you to look at things.' She picks out the manic energy and unique imagery of Gus Cummins's paintings and the strange, unsettling swimming-pool plaza paintings of Stephen Farthing. Also Jean Cooke's self-portrait, which Wilding reckons 'a very good likeness'. As Cockrill remarks, 'You've got to allow each painting to be effective – you can't kill it by putting something which is completely out of character too close to it.' He speaks eloquently of Fred Cuming's particular Englishness and Mary Fedden's 'objects in dialogue', Leonard McComb's beautiful and vibrantly patterned large portrait of Phillippa Cooper, and the subtle and restrained tempera paintings of David Tindle. It's impossible to mention everything, but highpoints include Adrian Berg's colour-filled visions of parkland and water; Anthony Eyton recording the construction of the geodesic domes of the Eden Project in Cornwall; the rugged symbolic landscape of Barbara Rae with its fierce colour contrasts; and Freddie Gore's two portraits – one of fellow Academician Gillian Ayres, the other of the sculptor Andrew Logan. Then there are Peter Coker's *Homage to John Singer Sargent*, Ivor Abrahams's huge rooster (opposite), Anthony Green on the inner life of objects, and Kitaj's extraordinary self-portrait as Old Father Time, his missing face framed by wild white hair and beard. Two large oils by Craigie Aitchison – a Crucifixion on red and a washing line in Italy – hang near Peter Blake's *Ophelia*. Gary Hume's painting *Young Nun*, a take on Cézanne's picture of the old maid in the National Gallery, hangs to the left of the doorway and acts as an introduction to Gallery IV, which is hung by him with work by artists he has asked to contribute to the Summer Exhibition.

Leonard McComb RA
Portrait of Phillippa Cooper
Oil
244 × 183 cm

Gary Hume RA
Young Nun
Gloss on aluminium
230 × 160 cm

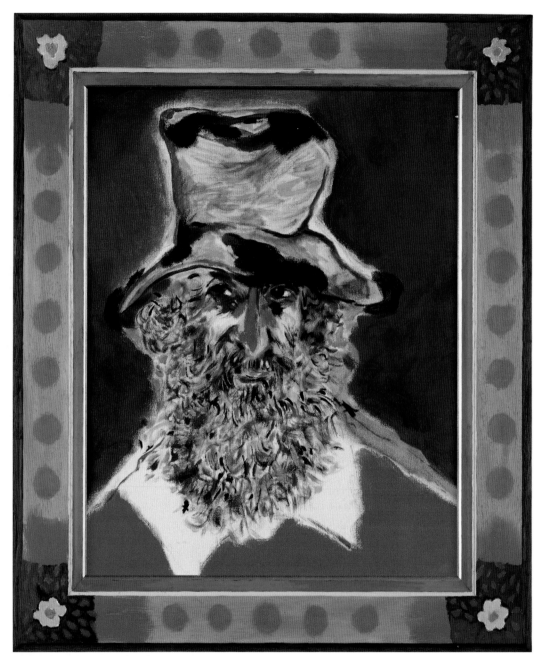

Philip Sutton RA
I am precisely as old as one should be!
Oil
81 × 68 cm

R.B. Kitaj RA
The Last of England (Self-portrait)
Oil
122 × 122 cm

John Wragg RA
Night's Pendulum
Jesmonite
H 87 cm

Stephen Farthing RA
Over the Path
Acrylic
41 × 51 cm

Ben Levene RA
Nocturne
Watercolour
28 × 37 cm

Frederick Gore CBE, RA
Andrew Logan, back from India
Oil
181 × 121 cm

Michael Rooney RA
El Cabrero
Oil
70 × 48 cm

Frederick Cuming RA
Harbour Entry. Clouds
Oil
90 × 90 cm

Dr. John Bellany CBE, RA
Macduff Sunset
Oil
90 × 90 cm

Anthony Green RA
The Edwardian Box and a Blue Vase
of Dried Yellow Flowers
Oil
50 × 26 cm

Mary Fedden OBE, RA
Duck's Breakfast
Oil
90 × 126 cm

Colin Hayes RA
Valley in Evvia, Greece
Oil
75 × 100 cm

Donald Hamilton Fraser RA
Montsegur
Oil
75 × 100 cm

Jeffery Camp RA
Stony Beach
Oil
28 × 28 cm

Eileen Cooper RA
Making an Entrance
Oil
123 × 91 cm

David Tindle RA
Open and Closed August Interior
Egg tempera
49 × 59 cm

Peter Coker RA
Homage to John Singer Sargent (The Daughters of Edward D. Boit)
Oil
90 × 90 cm

Adrian Berg RA
Stourhead 21st June 2001
Mixed media
29 × 89 cm

Prof. Norman Ackroyd RA
Connor Pass, Dingle Bay
Oil
62 × 50 cm

Prof. Brendan Neiland RA
Rerum Cognoscera Causas
Acrylic
185 × 124 cm

Antony Eyton RA
Malaysian Plants, Eden Project
Pastel
64 × 170 cm

Mick Moon RA
Tomato and Water
Monoprint
72 × 54 cm

Elizabeth Blackadder OBE, RA
Still Life and Japanese Chest
Oil
90 × 74 cm

Gus Cummins RA
Byway
Acrylic
177 × 127 cm

William Boyer RA
Lodge Road under Snow
Oil
91 × 120 cm

Jean E. Cooke RA
Self-portrait with Doves
Oil
62 × 72 cm

Gallery IV

Gary Hume's room is like a self-contained exhibition within the Summer Show, with a very definite personality. 'I sat down with my wife Georgie', he says, 'and made a list of artists to invite that I really admired. I asked for a piece of work that was really tough or something that they absolutely loved.' In another break with tradition, Hume has included a painting by Milton Avery, an American painter dead for nearly 40 years, whose work impressed him when he saw it recently. Usually, invited artists are among the living, but Avery's painting has such relevance to Hume's aesthetic that it was felt proper to admit it. Among the exhibits in this gallery are a paper cut-out by Simon Perriton of a broken cane chair, a painting of an opened-up rib cage by Nicola Tyson, a multi-coloured papier-mâché sculpture by the Austrian Franz West, a stark painting of coal and rubies by Dutchman Fons Haagmans, Don Brown's cast-plaster figure of a girl, Georgie Hopton's objects from a Picasso painting, and Rebecca Warren's reworking of Degas's young ballerina. Hume sees various themes emerging from the display, among them eroticism, references to art history, and the use of negative physical space. The work has a very distinct international flavour. The German Thomas Grunfeld comments on cloning with his mutant animals, this one a cross between a St Bernard and a sheep. Another Dutch artist, Daan van Golden, contributes a gorgeous blue-and-white painting of what to Hume looks like the profile of a budgie. Alison Wilding loves this painting: 'It's like a snowdrop.' She was also impressed by the Marlene Dumas painting because 'it's slightly creepy. It pulls you in but at the same time there's something repellent about it.' As Norman Rosenthal points out: 'Gary has become a very active member of the Royal Academy, and has taken a great interest in it. This is very encouraging for the future of the Academy which depends on new Members. Gary's selection presents a particular kind of colour and joyfulness.'

Rebecca Warren
Bunny
Unfired clay
H 60 cm

Daan van Golden
Study H.M. 2001
Oil
136 × 86 cm

Franz West
Untitled
Mixed media
H 190 cm

Marlene Dumas
Lovesick
Oil
50 × 60 cm

Gallery V

This gallery, and the following two, are filled with works selected by the Hanging Committee from the open submission. Hung by Gus Cummins, Gallery V has a professional, but not too solemn, feel to it. 'I think it's high time the Academy moved away from any slant towards the amateur,' says Cummins. 'Not that you don't get some wonderful amateur artists. For instance, a little garden painting by Irene Brooks-Baker has an extraordinary integrity and charm. It's not the sort of thing I was looking for, but it just impressed me. There's a marvellous Roy Oxlade called *Dotted Line 2*. The desert landscape next to it, *Karoo* by Yvonne Specktor, is very powerful; I'm quite envious of the beautiful paint, and if I see anything that I'm actually envious of, then that's a good day. The more I look into the rather strange, lyrically coloured painting by Angela Braven called *Homage to Nabokov*, the more I see. I was very pleased to put up the Dick Smiths from New York. I'm so glad that people of his calibre want to send in.' Cummins didn't set out to do such a sparse hang. 'If I had been overwhelmed by the quality of lots of small paintings, then that's what I'd have in. Of the small things I do have, there are three rather beautifully presented pieces by an artist I don't know, Malcolm Whittaker. On the other hand, there were some wonderful small landscapes sent in that were killed stone dead by the frames, which were either over-elaborate or the wrong colour, and which made them impossible to hang. A painting surface that I particularly like is Melanie Miller's extraordinary *Found Objects: White Flower and Secret* in oil on gesso. It has a gem-like quality that I'm interested in, almost like an icon.'

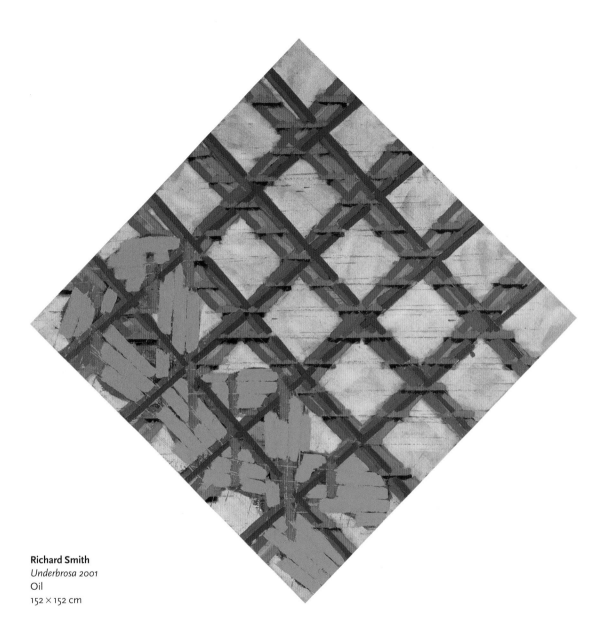

Richard Smith
Underbrosa 2001
Oil
152 × 152 cm

Rose Wylie
Tesco Label (Olive Oil) and Singer
Oil
183 × 180 cm

Melanie Miller
Found Objects: White Flowers and Secret
Oil
25 × 25 cm

Roy Oxlade
Dotted Line 2
Oil
133 × 172 cm

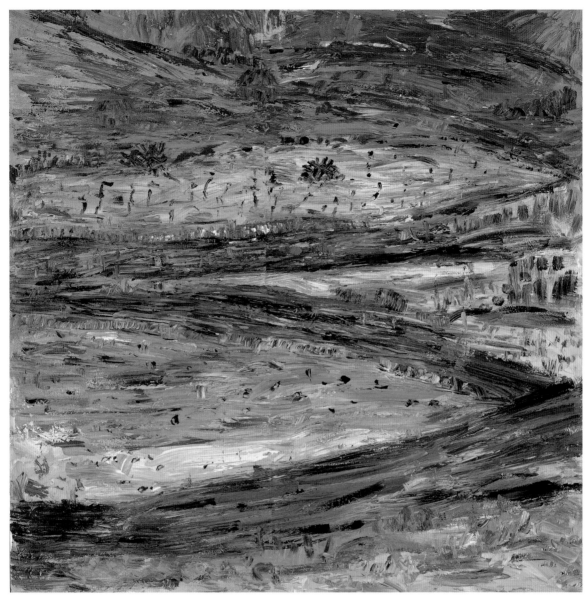

Yvonne Spektor
Karoo
Mixed media
182 × 186 cm

Susan Foord
Untitled
Mixed media
34 × 40 cm

Gallery VI

This is the second gallery of works from the open submission. Hung by Ken Howard, it is in some ways the most traditional of the galleries. 'My concept of the Summer Show is to hang the gallery as full as possible. There's no way you can turn the Summer Show into a Tate Modern show. There are some good names here even if they're not cutting-edge trendy. The main thing for me about painting is that it gives you a way of seeing. Every painter I select is doing that. I'm sure if I went from this gallery to Kensington Gardens this afternoon, I'd see it in terms of the Ruth Stage painting I've included. I always say that painting is about revelation, revealing the world to people; about communication, and I think all the paintings in this room will talk very directly to people when they come in; and about celebration, a celebration of life (as can be seen from the installation opposite). My other criterion is a very mundane one. Whenever I hang a picture I think "would I want to live with it?" I would be very pleased to go home and have my breakfast every morning under every picture in this room. Whether it's Peter Archer or Tom Fairs, Fred Dubery's Christmas tree, Karn Holly or Anthony Williams's egg-tempera still-lifes. The work I've hung is predominantly figurative though there are a number which are abstract; but finally every painting in this room is an abstract expression as well as a figurative one.'

Desmond Healy
In the Shadow of the Strand
Building – Lower Clapton Road
Charcoal
73 × 130 cm

Gabriela Schutz
Maze No. 4
Oil
27 × 45 cm

Gary McDonald
Allotments (Greenhouse)
Oil
25 × 31 cm

Karn Holly
Pool in the Dunes
Oil
118 × 147 cm

Gallery VII

This gallery, the third containing open-submission works, has been hung by Sonia Lawson. 'I've tried to get pictures that have some sort of freshness to them, not an academic recipe,' says Lawson. 'Art really is about re-creation, and although they're the same kind of subjects as any other year, I do feel there's a freshness, a "casual certainty" as Virginia Woolf described it. Most of the stuff I've chosen is abstract because it gives you that freedom to be creative without strings attached. Since the first time I was on the Hanging Committee in 1983 things have changed. There was a punk song then which went "Don't send me to art school, *please* don't send me to art school". Now, there's a lot more exciting work around and more risks are being taken. People have faith in art and the Summer Exhibition reaffirms this. All the old traditions are still underneath, and if people can build on these, you get something really exciting.' Alison Wilding particularly liked the two Mikey Cuddihy mixed-media drawings, Jeff Gibbons's 'fabulous' small drawing of a table, and Ivy Topham's *On the Edge*. Wilding further comments: 'Sonia Lawson has really taken on sculpture in her room in a way that none of the other painting galleries have. Here it has a real weight and presence.'

Jeff Gibbons
Table Would
Watercolour and pencil
36 × 26 cm

John Walker
Shade
Screenprint
23 × 26 cm

Ivy Topham
On the Edge
Brush and ink
49 × 69 cm

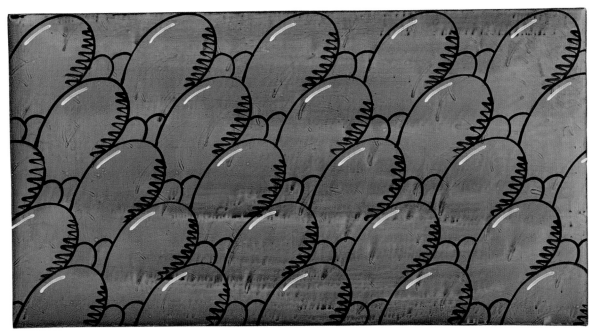

John Wilkins
I Stood Tall
Acrylic
75 × 142 cm

Franki Austin
Cloaked
Oil
107 × 76 cm

G.W. Bot
Entrance
Linocut
94 × 52 cm

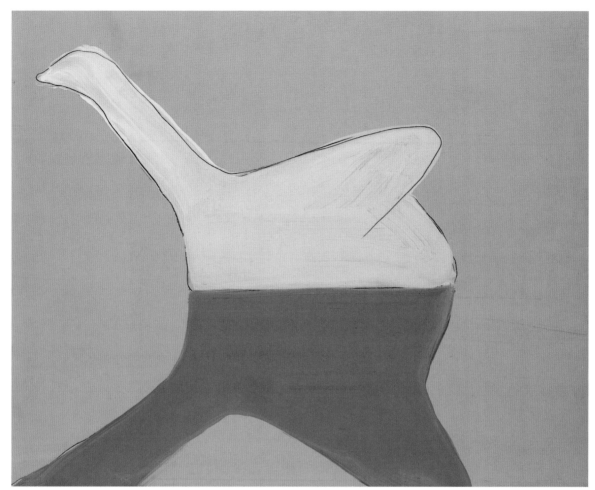

Miho Sato
Swan
Acrylic
61 × 72 cm

Wilhelmina Barns-Graham
Millennium Series Red II
Screenprint
24 × 31 cm

Mikey Cuddihy
Inventory Camden
Mixed media
116 × 81 cm

Gerard Hemsworth
Never mind, why?
Acrylic
213 × 244 cm

Kibog Park
Forked Road I
Oil
50 × 50 cm

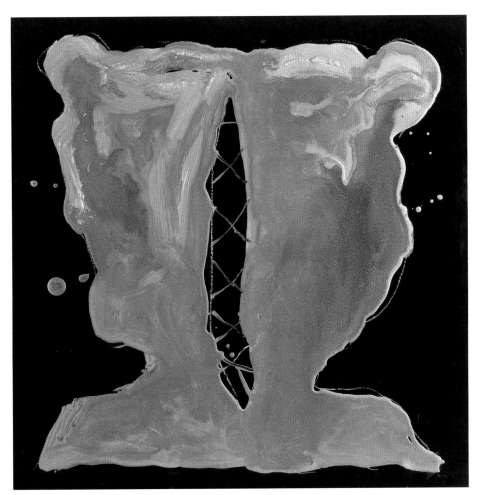

Madeleine Strindberg
Teddybear No 11
Oil
36 × 36 cm

Gallery VIII

Gallery VIII features the work of some of the Honorary RAs together with a huge four-part black-and-white landscape painting by John Virtue, purchased by the trustees of the Chantrey Bequest to be given to the Tate Gallery. There are works by Tàpies, Rauschenberg, Chillida and Baselitz. 'What is marvellous', says Norman Rosenthal, 'is that we have a very distinguished group of Honorary Members – some of the most famous painters and sculptors in the world. They add lustre to the exhibition.' The imposing Mimmo Paladino sculpture stands dramatically in the centre of the room (opposite). As Alison Wilding observes, it is a useful piece to have in a mixed exhibition, for it has something for everyone: it is both closed and open, and figurative as well as abstract. The strange Tàpies painting, with its cast-off clothing, chimes well with Rauschenberg's printed image of civilisation's detritus, hung at right angles to it. Frank Stella contributes a brightly painted metal wall-sculpture. Three heavily-structured Paladino paintings are variously interspersed. The Baselitz tondo follows, feet last.

John Virtue
Landscape 624
Mixed media
366 × 366 cm

Eduardo Chillida Hon RA
Hommage à Luis Bergarèche
Etching
159 × 123 cm

Frank Stella Hon RA
News of the Day
Mixed Media
H 94cm

Robert Rauschenberg Hon RA
Nest Egg
Mixed media
244 × 152 cm

Mimmo Paladino Hon RA
Euclide 2
Oil
250 × 195 cm

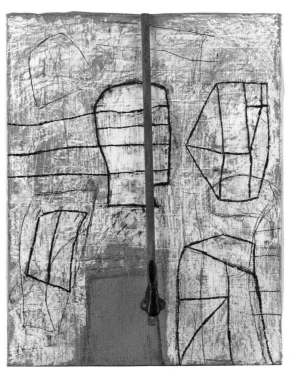

Mimmo Paladino Hon RA
Il Naso
Oil
81 × 65 cm

Gallery IX

Gallery IX is the first of the sculpture galleries. I asked Alison Wilding what her impressions were of the sculpture send-in this year. 'Probably the same as most years – a load of really dreadful stuff and some very unexpected things. Somehow you have to get both in. Inevitably it's a hotch-potch and an anachronism, but what's wrong with anachronisms? People enjoy them, and it's a very English event. There are some good things. Some of them are quite moving, like the little figures by Eleanor Edwards, *War and Peace* and *The Bull-Ringing*. But there aren't really that many non-RA participants in the sculpture section. In some ways it's more of a forum for RAs than an open submission. There seem to be three different categories: the RAs, the artists the RAs have asked to submit, and then the open submission. This year there are some very good invited artists, and I'm sure that's why the standard is up. Perhaps that's come to be more important than the open submission – particularly in sculpture.' Wilding's own piece is made of cast acrylic with carbon fragments suspended in it. It's a strange and beautiful object which is about solid and liquid at the same time. William Tucker's meteorite head fills the doorway and is clearly visible along the central axis through the three sculpture galleries. Wilding draws attention to certain exhibits: three dogs by Magnús Pálsson; a pair of flask-like bronze objects by Rachel Whiteread, apparently identical, one solid and weighing 25 kilos, the other hollow, like a skin. She praises Bryan Kneale's idea of placing the smaller sculptures on shelves rather than plinths. This has transformed the gallery, and rendered the hang infinitely more flexible and varied. ('Plinths are rather like coat-hangers,' says Kneale, 'they breed horribly.') Other works of note include Bill Woodrow's glove puppet; Ann Christopher's small, knife-like stainless-steel sculptures; Richard Deacon's tiny oval cardboard boxes, like plinths with curios sitting atop them; and a venerable Lynn Chadwick from 1956 entitled *208, Beast X*.

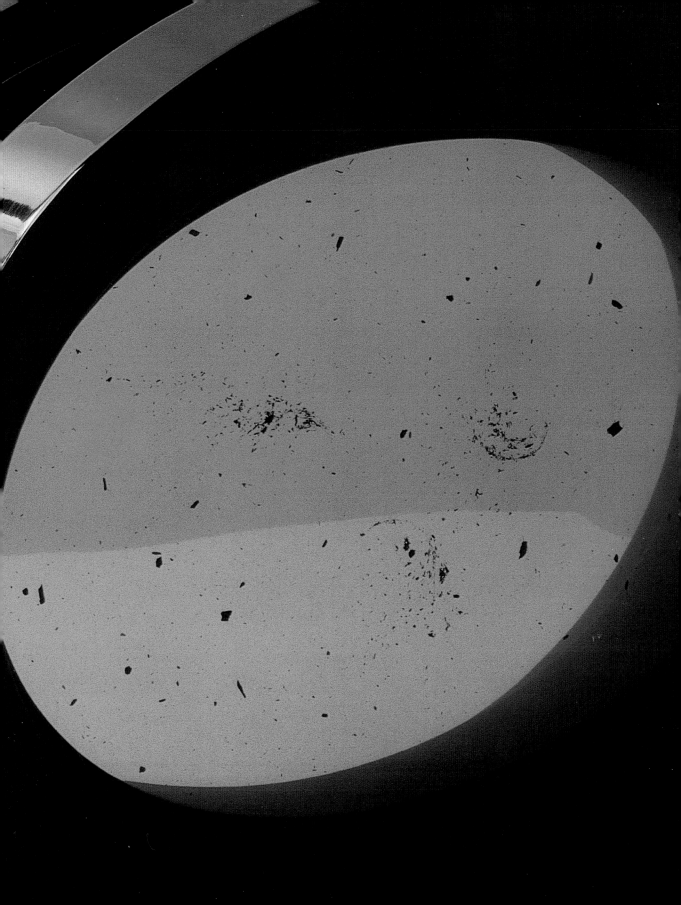

Paul de Monchaux
Volute
Bronze
H 39 cm

Sir Anthony Caro
Flageolet (Concerto Series) 1999
Wood, brass and bronze
H 47 cm

Georgeanne Slater
Malvolio
Marble
H 5 cm

William Tucker RA
Hero at Evening
Bronze
H 155 cm

Rachel Whiteread
Untitled, Empty and Full
Bronze
H 21 cm

Ann Christopher RA
Line of Light
Stainless steel
H 21 cm

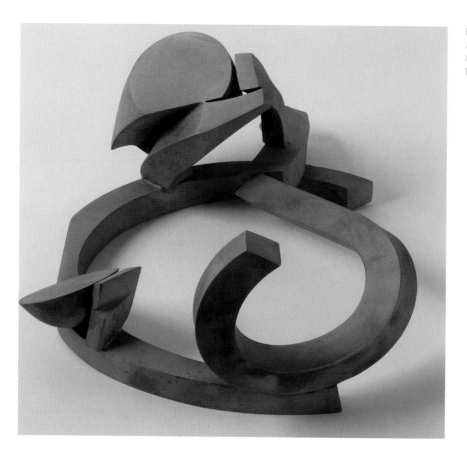

Prof. Bryan Kneale RA
Field
Brass
H 13 cm

Prof. Bryan Kneale RA
Castle
Brass
H 8 cm

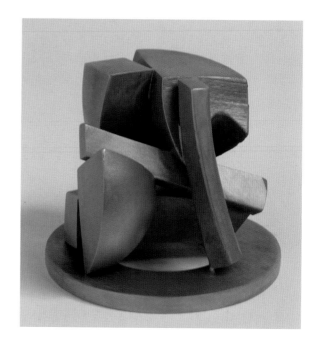

Prof. Sir Eduardo Paolozzi CBE, RA
Untitled
Bronze
H 39 cm

Harriet Aston
Little Body over Backwards
Glazed Clay
H 25 cm

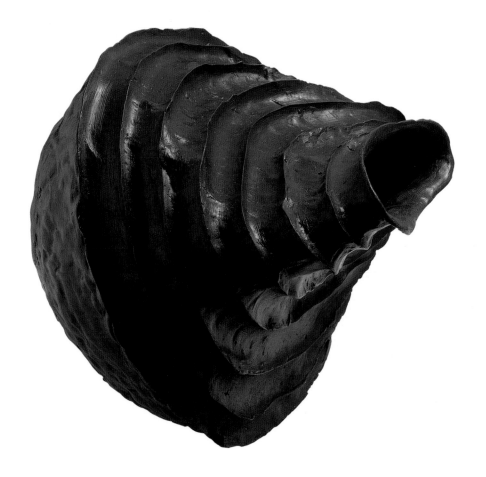

John Cobb
Domestic Improvement IV
Wood
H 36 cm

Richard Deacon CBE, RA
'C' 2000
Terracotta
H 24 cm

Alison Wilding RA
Flood Light
Cast acrylic and carbon
H 19 cm

Lynn Chadwick RA
208, Beast X, 1956
Bronze
H 25 cm

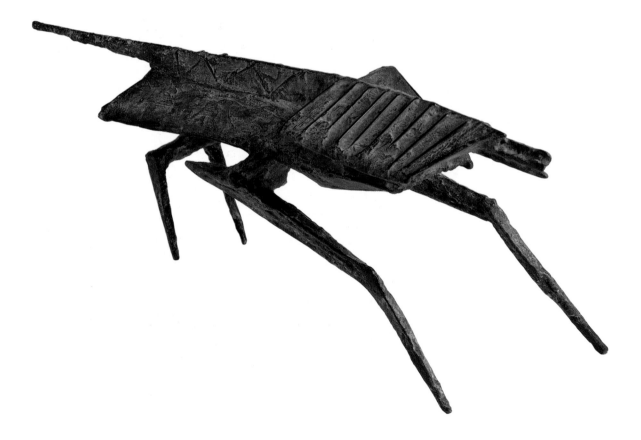

Prof. Christopher Le Brun RA
Fortune
Bronze
H 18 cm

Magnús Pálsson
Dog 3
Mixed media
H 44 cm

Nicola Hicks
Emperor 2002-05-16
Sand and Plaster
H 25 cm

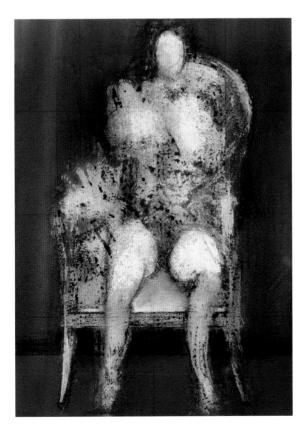

Robert Clatworthy RA
Seated Figure
Acrylic
37 × 27 cm

Steve Johnson
Deborah's Crown
Bronze
H 50 cm

Cathie Pilkington
Fair Isle
Jesmonite
H 73 cm

The Lecture Room is the second and largest gallery given over to sculpture, and it is hung with an admixture of paintings. A large, almost monochrome, painting by Anthony Whishaw makes a striking juxtaposition with three vertical wooden sculptures by David Nash. Elsewhere two of Whishaw's Japanese marsh paintings cast a gentle radiance. Wilding draws attention to two beautiful geometric wall-pieces by John Carter, one in greened bronze, the other painted in suave greys on plywood with acrylic and infusions of slate and marble powder. Two music pictures by Tom Phillips, the smaller a painting, the larger a pastel drawing, broadcast a silent but complex concert. The largest piece of sculpture in the room is *Within and Without II* by Nigel Hall, a double-bladed rusted corten-steel object, angled across the gallery within sight of his polished wood wall-piece in the Wohl Central Hall, itself setting up an interesting relationship, as Wilding points out, with the gilded roundel above it. A further intriguing sight-line relationship is set up with the heavy dark bronze of Barry Flanagan's thinking hare, which contrasts strikingly with the pale wood of Hall's sculpture, caught in flight against the wall. These are the kind of considerations which preoccupy the three-person sculpture hanging team of Bryan Kneale, Alison Wilding and Ann Christopher. As Wilding comments: 'The artists we have selected have enormously broadened the range of work in this room. For instance, Phyllida Barlow's curious table but not-table covered in thick gloopy paint. Or Eric Bainbridge's carefully arranged small geometrical constructions, made from plinth-like materials, which are an affectionate take on art history. Then there's Gavin Turk's bronze cardboard box which is so extraordinarily lifelike that no one believed it was a sculpture. It's a very mute, compelling object you really want to touch. The Marc Quinn photowork of an old woman with a baby in her arms was at first difficult to hang but placing it by the door made a strange but undeniable connection with the Tucker head.' Among the other distinguished pieces are Bill Woodrow's cello thronged with golden bees balanced on a rock (detail opposite), and Tony Cragg's three dynamic sculptures.

Anthony Cragg RA
Two Moods
Bronze
H 65 cm

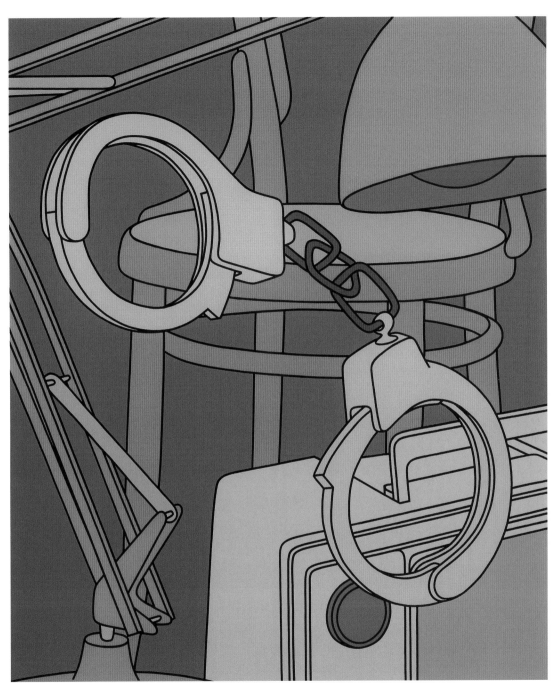

Michael Craig-Martin
Intimate Relations (detail)
Screenprint
80 × 96 cm

Geoffrey Clarke RA
M.S.W.R. IV
Acrylic and stone
34 × 55 cm

Phyllida Barlow
Neck
Mixed media
H 129 cm

John Carter
Triple Form 2002
Mixed media
76 × 207 cm

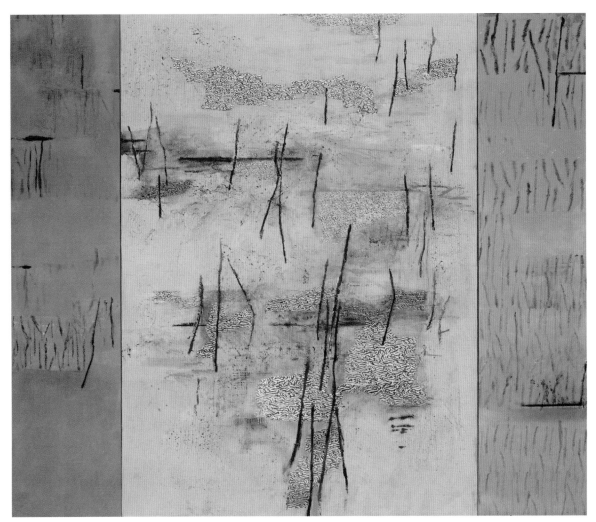

Anthony Whishaw RA
Marsh
Acrylic
168 × 199 cm

Nigel Hall
Within and Without
Corten steel
H 253 cm

David Nash RA
Crack & Warp Column in a Block
Elm
H 214 cm

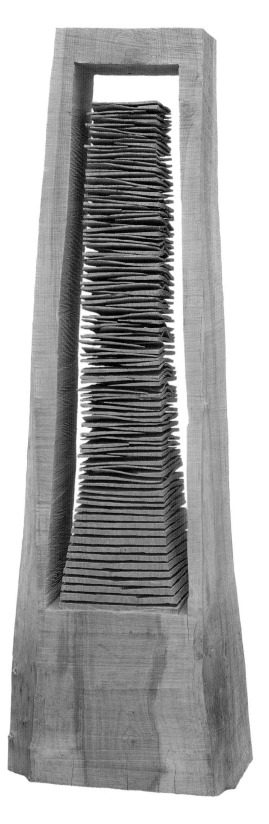

John Maine RA
Paradise Hill
Cast iron
H 8 cm

John Maine RA
Hill top
Bronze
H 15 cm

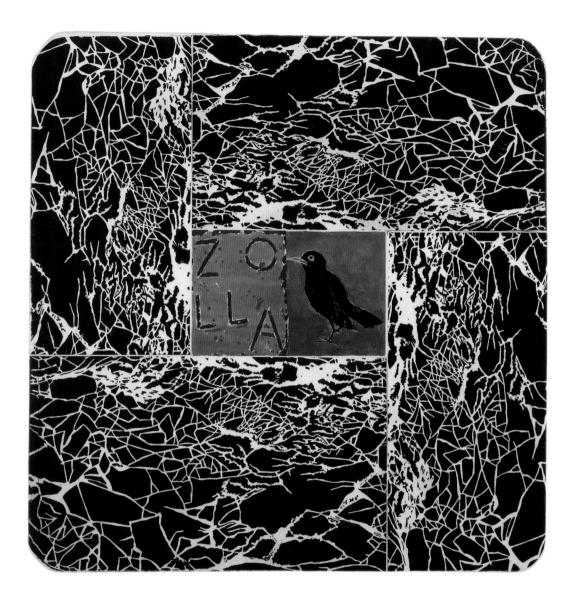

Joe Tilson RA
Conjunction Blackbird, Zolla
Mixed media
85 × 82 cm

B.E. Cole
Form
Aluminium
H 240 cm

Flavia Irwin RA
Perceptual Comment 2
Watercolour
102 × 71 cm

Wohl Central Hall

The octagonal Wohl Central Hall is the culmination of the sculpture galleries. Too often it is the repository of the pictures and sculptures that didn't fit anywhere else, but this year, the selectors have been severe about what is hung here, and as Bryan Kneale remarks 'we've tried to make it a temple of elegance and clarity, of perfect placing'. A Richard Long text piece about a fifteen-day walk in Oregon hangs above the main tribute to Kenneth Armitage who died this year (installation opposite). His inventive figure-based sculptures evoke a previous era redolent of Cold War anxieties. A melted gilt head by Bill Woodrow surmounted by a beehive alludes to the risks of apiarism, while Ann Christopher's large, meticulously made blade, despite its verticality, has an aerodynamic quality. A group of four Ken Draper wall-sculptures hint at hidden places and warmer climates. Two extended landscape sculptures by Bryan Kneale recall a fifteen-foot three-dimensional map of the Isle of Man in the Manx Museum. Kneale grew up on the island, and these sculptures evoke childhood memories of hills and valleys and looking out to sea. They also refer to his lifelong interest in Celtic smithery and his love of Paul Nash's great painting of crashed aircraft, *Totes Meer*.

HEAVEN AND EARTH

MOVING BY DAY RESTING BY NIGHT
GLACIER CREEK GLITTERING WATER GLITTERING OBSIDIAN
EACH SLEEPING PLACE THE DREAMS AT EACH SLEEPING PLACE
NORTH SISTER KICKING IN SNOW-STEPS *WICKIUP PLAIN* EASY WALKING
AN ODD NUMBER OF MOUNTAINS AN EVEN NUMBER OF RIVERS
THE EARTH'S AXIS MAGNETIC NORTH POSITIVE MAGNETIC SOUTH NEGATIVE
THE WALK AS A TRUE PATH SOME FALSE MOVES

A 15 DAY WALK IN THE THREE SISTERS WILDERNESS OREGON 2001

The late Kenneth Armitage CBE, RA
Pandarus
Brass
H 190 cm

Bill Woodrow
Self-portrait in the Year 2002
Mixed media
H 51 cm

Kenneth Draper RA
Imminent Eclipse 2002
Mixed media
H 118 cm

Kenneth Draper RA
Night Reflections/Egypt
Mixed media
H 56 cm

Gallery X

This is the architecture room, this year hung by Will Alsop, Lord Foster and Michael Manser. Alsop comments: 'As usual, the problem with this room is that architecture comes in all shapes and sizes, and completely different styles, which you could argue does reflect what's going on at the moment. There's no predominant style, no predominant theory. Presentation is a terrible problem. When left to their own devices, architects do stupid things like mount their entries on bits of stainless steel. Some want to show straightforward architectural drawings – a plan or a section, but they should be framed very simply in black or wood. Unlike painters, generally speaking, architects don't think about the frame in relationship to the work. So this year we're concentrating on the models, and putting them all at eye level, which allows you to disappear into their Lilliputian worlds. The send-in was probably 75–80% disappointing. We could have filled the room with Members' work only. The mixture we've actually hung is probably 60% Members, 40% non-Members.' Among the things that Alsop singled out are an Eric Parry drawing for the Turner Centre, Margate; a drawing of the roof structure for the Graz Kunsthaus by Peter Cook; and a model by the bright young practice of Birds Portchmouth and Russum of two red bridges, one lifting, one swinging. Michael Manser is more optimistic about the selection. Among the models he pointed out are Lord Rogers's Silvertown Dock and the towers for Madrid; Lord Foster's Business Academy at Bexley; and Eva Jiricna's penthouse flat for Canary Wharf.

Paul Koralek CBE, RA (Ahrends, Burton & Koralek Architects)
A tall building for Dublin
Print
37 × 28 cm

Prof. Gordon Benson CBE, RA
National Gallery of Ireland (detail)
Photograph
58 × 191 cm

Prof. William Alsop RA
Goldsmiths Two
Digital print
53 × 79 cm

Edward Cullinan CBE, RA
Plan of Turner Gallery, Margate
Digital print
42 × 80 cm

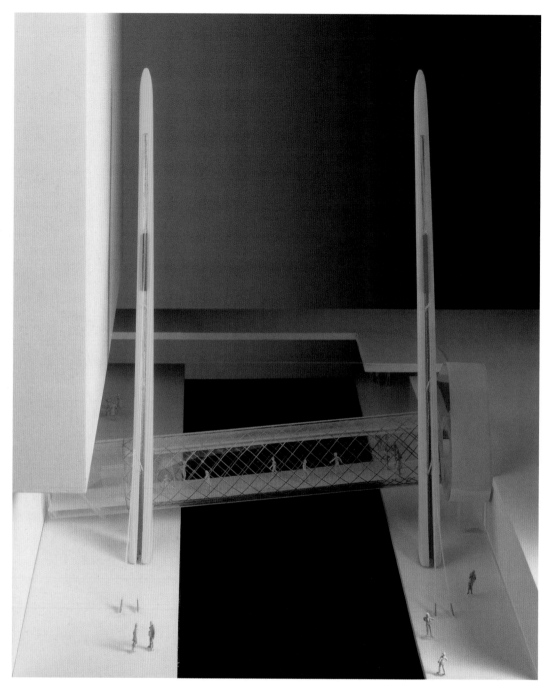

Eva Jiricna CBE, RA (Eva Jiricna Architects)
Bellmouth Pedestrian Bridge, Canary Wharf
Model
H 60 cm

Lord Rogers of Riverside RA (Richard Rogers Partnership)
Torre Espacio, Madrid, Spain
Model
H 60 cm

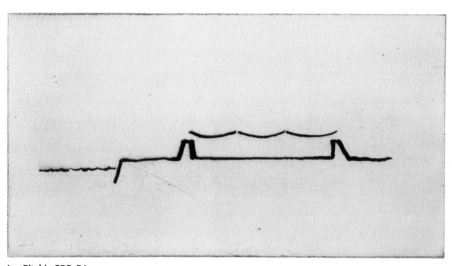

Ian Ritchie CBE, RA
London Regatta Centre
Etching
12 × 24 cm

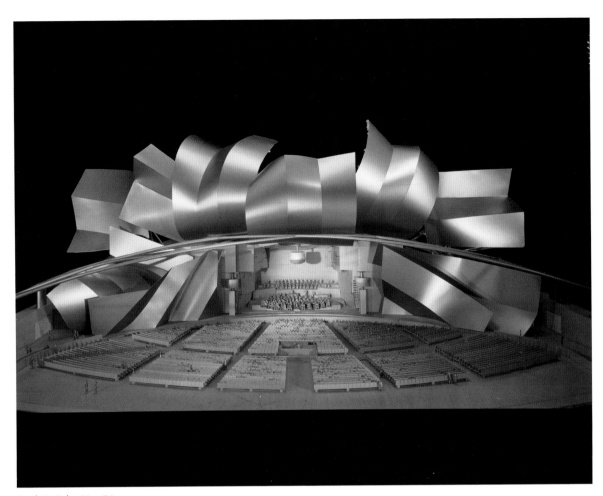

Frank O. Gehry Hon RA
Millennium Park Music Pavillion
Photograph
71 × 89 cm

Leonard Manasseh OBE, RA
Addition to a house by others,
No 6, view from the garden
Laserprint
30 × 39 cm

Prof. Trevor Dannatt RA (Dannatt, Johnson Architects)
University of Westminster, Marylebone Campus (detail)
Photograph
73 × 59 cm

Tennant Room

Hung by Tom Phillips as a footnote or coda to the Summer Exhibition, the Tennant Room is a moving homage to Sir Ernst Gombrich, an Honorary Fellow, who died last year. Each work has a special meaning and relevance to the life and interests of this great art historian, centring around his magisterial portrait by R. B. Kitaj, borrowed from the National Portrait Gallery. Every exhibit has been carefully selected by Phillips to propose an argument or make a point that Gombrich would have appreciated. For instance, the suspended Antony Gormley sculpture is there to cast a shadow, referring to the exhibition about shadows in art that Gombrich curated for the National Gallery. The room as a whole is called 'eg', spelling out both 'for example' and Gombrich's initials, the letters designed on two panels by Tom Phillips in appropriately decorative style. Ornament and repetition were a preoccupation of Gombrich's, hence also the inclusion of a tower sculpture by John Maine. David Hockney is represented by a flower painting, since with his new theories about optics and the *camera obscura* he has now himself joined the ranks of art historians. A complex drawing by Victor Newsome containing some 16 points of perspective contrasts effectively with Sandra Blow's abstraction, but both reflect Gombrich's interests, one in traditional perspective systems, the other in a kind of modern equivalent of a painter of 'the floating world', with no apparent programme but immense style and eloquence. Tom Phillips's main contribution is a piece about Dada, bearing the legend (in German) 'take Dada seriously, it's worth it'. It's an affectionate dig at Gombrich's denigration of modern art, while also referring obliquely to his book *Meditations on a Hobby Horse* (1963), for the German word 'dada' actually means hobby horse. A multi-layered and richly allusive celebration of a remarkable scholar.

David Hockney CH, RA
Violet in Front of Plan Chest
Oil
66 × 81cm

John Maine RA
Pinnacle
Cast Aluminium
H 180 cm

Index

Royal Academy of Arts in London, 2002

Royal Academy Trust

Registered charity number 1067270

The Royal Academy of Arts, Registered Charity number 212798, is Britain's founding society for promoting the creation and appreciation of the visual arts through exhibitions, education and debate. Independently led by eminent artists and architects, the Royal Academy receives no annual funding via the government, and is entirely reliant on self-generated income and charitable support.

You and/or your company can support the Royal Academy of Arts in a number of different ways:

- £20 million has been raised for capital projects, including the Jill and Arthur M Sackler Wing, the restoration of the Main Galleries and the redesign of the courtyard.
- Future projects include the restoration of the Fine Rooms, and the provision of better facilities for the display and enjoyment of the Academy's own Collections of important works of art and documents charting the history of British art.
- Donations from individuals, trusts, companies and foundations also help support the Academy's internationally renowned exhibition programme, the conversation of the Collections and educational projects for schools, families and people with special needs; as well as providing scholarships and bursaries for postgraduate art students in the RA Schools.
- Companies invest in the Royal Academy through arts sponsorship, corporate membership and corporate entertaining, with specific opportunities that relate to your budgets and marketing/entertaining objectives.

- A legacy is perhaps the most personal way to make a lasting contribution, through the Trust endowment fund, ensuring that the enjoyment you have derived is guaranteed for future generations.

To find out ways in which individuals, trusts and foundations can support this work (or a specific aspect), please contact Vanessa Bowcock on 020 7300 5698 to discuss your personal interests and wishes.

To explore ways in which companies can become involved in the work of the Academy to mutual benefit, please telephone Pamela Carswell on 020 7300 5705.

To discuss leaving a legacy to the Royal Academy of Arts, please telephone Sally Johnson 020 7300 5677.

Membership of the Friends

Registered charity number 272926

The Friends of the Royal Academy was founded in 1977 to support and promote the work of the Royal Academy. It is now one of the largest such organisations in the world, with over 80,000 individual members. Friends' donations contribute around 20% of the RA's total annual income.

As a Friend you enjoy free entry to every RA exhibition and much more...

- Visit exhibitions as often as you like, bypassing ticket queues
- Bring an adult guest and four children, all free

- See exhibitions first at previews
- Keep up to date through RA Magazines
- Have access to the Friends Room

Why not join today

- Onsite at the Friends desks in the Front Hall
- Online on www.royalacademy.org.uk
- Ring 020 7300 5664 any day of the week

Support the foremost UK organisation for promoting the visual arts and architecture – which receives no regular government funding. *Please also ask about Gift Aid.*

Editorial co-ordinators:
Carola Krueger and Nick Tite
Design: 01.02
Cover: Allen Jones RA, *Refrigerator*
(detail).
Photograph by Erik Hesmerg
Colour reproduction:
DawkinsColour
Photography: FXP Photography
and John Riddy
Printed in Italy

ISBN 1 903973 10 4

Illustrations

Page 2: Albert Irvin RA, *Schubert 2002* (detail)
Page 6: The Wohl Central Hall, showing works by Barry Flanagan RA and Nigel Hall
Page 9: Allen Jones RA, *Refrigerator*
Page 12: Prof. Phillip King CBE PRA, *And did those hills...* (detail)
Page 21: Gallery II, showing works by Maurice Cockrill RA and Sir Kyffin Williams OBE RA
Page 33: Peter Blake CBE RA, *Stanley Road* (detail)
Page 61: Allen Jones RA, *Light Orange* (detail)
Page 65: Gallery III, showing *Cockerel* by Ivor Abrahams RA
Page 93: Gallery IV, showing works by Marlene Dumas, Thomas Grunfeld, Don Brown and Alan Charlton
Page 99: Gallery V, showing a detail of *Serie Accident de Chasse le Jaguar* by Pascal Bernier
Page 111: Wilhelmina Barns-Graham, *Millennium Series Red II* (detail)
Page 125: Gallery VIII, showing *Donna 2000* by Mimmo Paladino Hon RA in the foreground
Page 133: Alison Wilding RA, *Flood Light* (detail)
Page 153: Installation of Lecture Room with detail of *Cello Swarm* by Bill Woodrow
Page 167: The Wohl Central Hall, showing works by Ann Christopher RA, the late Kenneth Armitage CBE RA and Richard Long RA
Page 173: Detail of Capital City Academy, Brent, by Lord Foster of Thames Bank OM RA (Foster and Partners)
Page 185: Tom Phillips RA, *E.G. (Title Piece after Wittgenstein)* (detail)

Photographic Acknowledgements

Page 94: Courtesy of Maureen Paley Interim Art, London
Pages 125, 130, 131: Courtesy of Waddington Galleries
Page 128: Courtesy of Bernard Jacobson Gallery; © ARS, NY and DACS, London 2002
Page 154: Courtesy of Galerie Buchmann; photo by Niels Schabrod
Page 181: © Gehry Partners, LLP; Photo Whit Preston
Page 183: Photo Peter Cook